Also by Tony Harrison

Selected Poems (1987)

V. and Other Poems

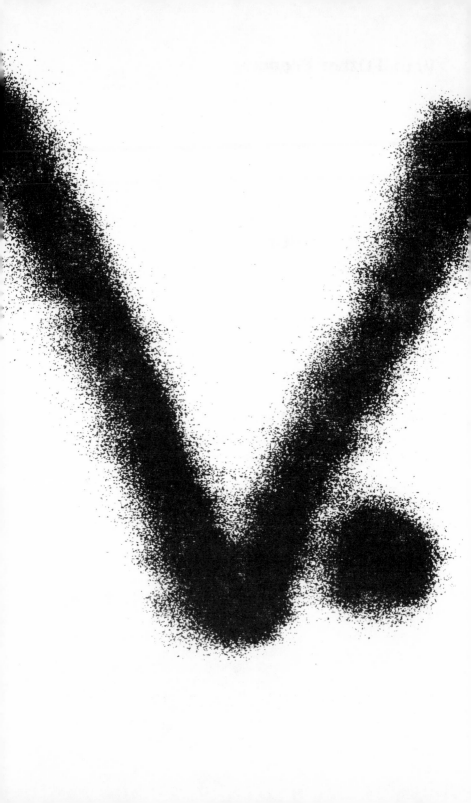

and Other Poems

Tony Harrison

Farrar Straus Giroux

New York

The author would like to acknowledge the
following, where many of these poems first
appeared: *London Review of Books, The Observer,
Poetry Review, The Times Literary Supplement.*
The author would also like to acknowledge the
Scargill Press for their publication of "Sonnets for
August 1945" in *Anno Forty-Two*, and Anvil Press
for their publication of "Changing at York" in *10
Sonnets from 'The School of Eloquence.'*

Contents

V. and Other Poems

American Poems

V. and Other Poems

V.

*'My father still reads the dictionary every
day. He says your life depends on your
power to master words.'*

> —ARTHUR SCARGILL
> *The Sunday Times*, 10 Jan. 1982

Next millennium you'll have to search quite hard
to find my slab behind the family dead,
butcher, publican and baker, now me, bard
adding poetry to their beef, beer and bread.

With Byron three graves on I'll not go short
of company, and Wordsworth's opposite.
That's two peers already, of a sort,
and we'll all be thrown together if the pit,

whose galleries once ran beneath this plot,
causes the distinguished dead to drop
into the rabblement of bone and rot,
shored slack, crushed shale, smashed prop.

Wordsworth built church organs, Byron tanned
luggage cowhide in the age of steam,
and knew their place of rest before the land
caves in on the lowest worked-out seam.

This graveyard on the brink of Beeston Hill's
the place I may well rest if there's a spot
under the rose roots and the daffodils
by which Dad dignified the family plot.

If buried ashes saw then I'd survey
the places I learned Latin, and learned Greek,
and left, the ground where Leeds United play
but disappoint their fans week after week,

which makes them lose their sense of self-esteem
and taking a shortcut home through these graves here
they reassert the glory of their team
by spraying words on tombstones, pissed on beer.

This graveyard stands above a worked-out pit.
Subsidence makes the obelisks all list.
One leaning left's marked FUCK, one right's marked SHIT
sprayed by some peeved supporter who was pissed.

Farsighted for his family's future dead,
but for his wife, this banker's still alone
on his long obelisk, and doomed to head
a blackened dynasty of unclaimed stone,

now graffitied with a crude four-letter word.
His children and grandchildren went away
and never came back home to be interred
so left a lot of space for skins to spray.

The language of this graveyard ranges from
a bit of Latin for a former mayor
or those who laid their lives down at the Somme,
the hymnal fragments and the gilded prayer,

how people 'fell asleep in the Good Lord,'
brief chisellable bits from the good book
and rhymes whatever length they could afford
to CUNT, PISS, SHIT and (mostly) FUCK!

or, more expansively, there's LEEDS v.
the opponent of last week, this week, or next,
and a repertoire of blunt four-letter curses
on the team or race that makes the sprayer vexed.

Then, rushed for time, or fleeing some observer,
dodging between tall family vaults and trees,
like his team's best-ever winger, dribbler, swerver,
fills every space he finds with versus Vs.

Vs sprayed on the run at such a lick,
the sprayer master of his flourished tool,
get short-armed on the left like that red tick
they never marked his work much with at school.

Half this skinhead's age but with approval
I helped whitewash a V on a brick wall.
No one clamoured in the press for its removal
or thought the sign, in wartime, rude at all.

These Vs are all the versuses of life
from LEEDS v. DERBY, Black/White
and (as I've known to my cost) man v. wife,
Communist v. Fascist, Left v. Right,

class v. class as bitter as before,
the unending violence of US and THEM,
personified in 1984
by Coal Board MacGregor and the N.U.M.,

Hindu/Sikh, soul/body, heart v. mind,
East/West, male/female, and the ground
these fixtures are fought out on's Man, resigned
to hope from his future what his past never found.

The prospects for the present aren't too grand
when a swastika with NF (National Front)'s
sprayed on a grave, to which another hand
has added, in a reddish colour, CUNTS.

Which is, I grant, the word that springs to mind
when, going to clear the weeds and rubbish thrown
on the family grave by football fans, I find
UNITED graffitied on my parents' stone.

How many British graveyards now this May
are strewn with rubbish and choked up with weeds
since families and friends have gone away
for work or fuller lives, like me, from Leeds?

When I first came here 40 years ago
with my dad to 'see' my grandma I was 7.
I helped Dad with the flowers. He let me know
she'd gone to join my granddad up in Heaven.

My dad who came each week to bring fresh flowers
came home with clay stains on his trouser knees.
Since my parents' deaths I've spent 2 hours
made up of odd 10 minutes such as these,

Flying visits once or twice a year,
and though I'm horrified, just who's to blame
that I find instead of flowers cans of beer
and more than one grave sprayed with some skin's name?

Where there were flower urns and troughs of water
and mesh receptacles for withered flowers
are the HARP tins of some skinhead Leeds supporter.
It isn't all his fault, though. Much is ours.

5 kids, with one in goal, play 2-a-side.
When the ball bangs on the hawthorn that's one post
and petals fall they hum 'Here Comes the Bride'
though not so loud they'd want to rouse a ghost.

They boot the ball on purpose at the trunk
and make the tree shed showers of shrivelled may.
I look at this word graffitied by some drunk
and I'm in half a mind to let it stay.

(Though honesty demands that I say *if*
I'd wanted to take the necessary pains
to scrub the skin's inscription off
I only had an hour between trains.

So the feelings that I had as I stood gazing
and the significance I saw could be a sham,
mere excuses for not patiently erasing
the word sprayed on the grave of Dad and Mam.)

This pen's all I have of magic wand.
I know this world's so torn but want no other
except for Dad who'd hoped from 'the Beyond'
a better life than this one *with* my mother.

Though I don't believe in afterlife at all
and know it's cheating, it's hard not to make
a sort of furtive prayer from this skin's scrawl,
his UNITED means 'in Heaven' for their sake,

an accident of meaning to redeem
an act intended as mere desecration
and make the thoughtless spraying of his team
apply to higher things, and to the nation.

Some, where kids use aerosols, use giant signs
to let the people know who's forged their fetters
like PRI   CE   O   WALES above West Yorkshire mines
(no prizes for who nicked the missing letters!)

The big blue star for booze, tobacco ads,
the magnate's monogram, the royal crest,
insignia in neon dwarf the lads
who spray a few odd FUCKs when they're depressed.

Letters of transparent tubes and gas
in Dusseldorf are blue and flash out KRUPP.
Arms are hoisted for the British ruling class
and clandestine, genteel aggro keeps them up.

And there's HARRISON on some Leeds building sites
I've taken in fun as blazoning my name,
which I've also seen on books, in Broadway lights,
so why can't skins with spray cans do the same?

But why inscribe these *graves* with CUNT and SHIT?
Why choose neglected tombstones to disfigure?
This pitman's of last century daubed PAKI GIT,
this grocer Broadbent's aerosoled with NIGGER?

They're there to shock the living, not arouse
the dead from their deep peace to lend support
for any cause skins' spray cans could espouse.
The dead would want their desecrators caught!

Jobless though they are how can these kids,
even though their team's lost one more game,
believe that the 'Pakis,' 'Niggers,' even 'Yids'
sprayed on the tombstones here should take the blame?

What is it that these crude words are revealing?
What is it that this aggro act implies?
Giving the dead their xenophobic feeling
or just a *cri-de-coeur* because Man dies.

So what's a cri-de-coeur, *cunt? Can't yer speak*
the language that yer mam spoke? Think of 'er!
Can yer only get yer tongue round fucking Greek?
Go and fuck yerself with cri-de-coeur!

'She didn't talk like you do for a start!'
I shouted, turning where I thought the voice had been.
She didn't understand yer fucking art!
She thought yer fucking poetry obscene!

I wish on this skin's word deep aspirations,
first the prayer for my parents I can't make,
then a call to Britain and to all the nations
made in the name of love for peace's sake.

Aspirations, cunt! Folk on t' fucking dole
'ave got about as much scope to aspire
above the shit they're dumped in, cunt, as coal
aspires to be chucked on t' fucking fire.

O.K., forget the aspirations! Look, I know
United's losing gets you fans incensed
and how far the HARP inside you makes you go
but all these Vs: against! against! against!

Ah'll tell yer then what really riles a bloke.
It's reading on their graves the jobs they did—
butcher, publican and baker. Me, I'll croak
doing t' same nowt ah do now as a kid.

'ard birth ah wor, mi mam says, almost killed 'er.
Death after life on t' dole won't seem as 'ard!
Look at this cunt, Wordsworth, organ builder,
this fucking 'aberdasher, Appleyard!

If mi mam's up there, don't want to meet 'er
listening to me list mi dirty deeds
and 'ave to pipe up to St. fucking Peter
ah've been on t' dole all mi life in fucking Leeds.

Then t' Alleluias stick in t' angels' gobs.
When dole-wallahs fuck off to the void
what'll t' mason carve up for their jobs?
The cunts who lieth 'ere wor unemployed?

This lot worked at one job all life through.
Byron, 'Tanner,' Lieth 'ere interred!
They'll chisel fucking poet when they do you
and that, yer cunt, 's a crude four-letter word.

'Listen, cunt!' I said, 'before you start your jeering,
the reason why I want this in a book
's to give ungrateful cunts like you a hearing!'
A book, yer stupid cunt, 's not worth a fuck!

'The only reason why I write this poem at all
on yobs like you who do the dirt on death
's to give some higher meaning to your scrawl!'
Don't fucking bother, cunt! Don't waste your breath!

'You piss-artist skinhead cunt, you wouldn't know
and it doesn't fucking matter if you do,
the skin and poet united fucking Rimbaud
but the *autre* that *je est* is fucking you.'

Ah've told yer, no more Greek. That's yer last warning!
Ah'll boot yer fucking balls to Kingdom Come.
They'll find yer cold on t' grave tomorrer morning.
So don't speak Greek. Don't treat me like I'm dumb.

'I've done my bits of mindless aggro too
not half a mile from where we're standing now.'
Yeah, ah bet yer wrote a poem, yer wanker you!
'No, shut yer gob awhile. Ah'll tell yer 'ow . . .

'Herman Darewski's band played operetta
with a wobbly soprano warbling. Just why
I made my mind up that I'd got to get her
with the fire hose I can't say, but I'll try.

'It wasn't just the singing angered me.
At the same time half a crowd was jeering
as the smooth Hugh Gaitskell, our MP,
made promises the other half was cheering.

'What I hated in those high soprano ranges
was uplift beyond all reason and control
and in a world where you say nothing changes
it seemed a sort of prick-tease of the soul.

'I tell you when I heard high notes that rose
above Hugh Gaitskell's cool electioneering
straight from the warbling throat right up my nose,
I had all your aggro in *my* jeering.

'And I hit the fire extinguisher ON knob
and covered orchestra and audience with spray.
I could run as fast as you then. A good job!
They yelled 'Damned vandal' after me that day . . .'

And then yer saw the light and gave up 'eavy
And knew a man's not 'ow much 'e can sup . . .
Yer reward for growing up's this super-bevvy,
a meths and champagne punch in t'FA Cup.

Ah've 'eard all that from old farts past their prime.
'ow now yer live wi' all yer once detested . . .
Old farts wi' not much left'll give me time.
Fuckers like that get folk like me arrested.

Covet not thy neighbour's wife, thy neighbour's riches.
Vicar and cop who say, to save our souls:
Get thee behind me, Satan! *drop* their *breeches*
and get the Devil's dick right up their 'oles!

It was more a working marriage that I'd meant,
a blend of masculine and feminine.
Ignoring me, he started looking, bent
on some more aerosoling, for his tin.

'It was more a working marriage that I mean!'
Fuck, and save mi soul, eh? That suits me.
Then as if I'd egged him on to be obscene
he added a middle slit to one daubed V.

Don't talk to me of fucking representing
the class yer were born into anymore.
Yer going to get 'urt and start resenting
it's not poetry we need in this class war.

Yer've given yerself toffee, cunt. Who needs
yer fucking poufy words. Ah write mi own.
Ah've got mi work on show all over Leeds
like this UNITED *'ere on some sod's stone.*

'O.K.!' (thinking I had him trapped). 'O.K.!'
'If you're so proud of it then sign your name
when next you're full of HARP and armed with spray,
next time you take this shortcut from the game.'

He took the can, contemptuous, unhurried,
and cleared the nozzle and prepared to sign
the UNITED sprayed where Mam and Dad were buried.
He aerosoled his name, and it was mine.

The boy footballers bawl 'Here Comes the Bride'
and drifting blossoms fall onto my head.
One half of me's alive but one half died
when the skin half sprayed my name among the dead.

Half versus half, the enemies within
the heart that can't be whole till they unite.
As I stoop to grab the crushed HARP lager tin
the day's already dusk, half dark, half light.

The UNITED that I'd wished onto the nation
or as reunion for dead parents soon recedes.
The word's once more a mindless desecration
by some HARPoholic yob supporting Leeds.

Almost the time for ghosts. I'd better scram.
Though not given much to fears of spooky scaring
I don't fancy an encounter with mi mam
playing Hamlet with me for this swearing.

Though I've a train to catch my step is slow.
I walk on the grass and graves with wary tread
over the subsidences, these shifts below
the life of Leeds supported by the dead.

Further underneath's that cavernous hollow
that makes the gravestones lean towards the town.
A matter of mere time and it will swallow
this place of rest and all the resters down.

I tell myself I've got, say, 30 years.
At 75 this place will suit me fine.
I've never feared the grave but what I fear's
that great worked-out black hollow under mine.

Not train departure time and not Town Hall
with the great white clock face I can see,
coal, that began, with no man here at all,
as 300-million-year-old plant debris.

5 kids still play at making blossoms fall
and humming as they do 'Here Comes the Bride.'
They never seem to tire of their ball
though I hear a woman's voice call one inside.

2 larking boys play bawdy bride and groom.
3 boys in Leeds strip la-la *Lohengrin*.
I hear them as I go through growing gloom
still years away from being skald or skin.

The ground's carpeted with petals as I throw
the aerosol, the HARP can, the cleared weeds
on top of Dad's dead daffodils, then go,
with not one glance behind away from Leeds.

The bus to the station's still the No. 1
but goes by routes that I don't recognize.
I look out for known landmarks as the sun
reddens the swabs of cloud in darkening skies.

Home, home, home, to my woman as the red
darkens from a fresh blood to a dried.
Home, home to my woman, home to bed
where opposites are sometimes unified.

A pensioner in turban taps his stick
along the pavement past the corner shop,
that sells samosas now not beer on tick,
to the Kashmir Muslim Club that was the Co-op.

House after house FOR SALE where we'd played cricket
with white roses cut from flour sacks on our caps,
with stumps chalked on the coal grate for our wicket,
and every one bought now by 'coloured chaps,'

Dad's most liberal label as he felt
squeezed by the unfamiliar, and fear
of foreign food and faces, when he smelt
curry in the shop where he'd bought beer.

And growing frailer, 'wobbly on his pins,'
the shops he felt familiar with withdrew
which meant much longer tiring treks for tins
that had a label on them that he knew.

And as the shops that stocked his favourites receded
whereas he'd fancied beans and popped next door,
he found that four long treks a week were needed
till he wondered what he bothered eating for.

The supermarket made him feel embarrassed.
Where people bought whole lambs for family freezers
he bought baked beans from checkout girls too harassed
to smile or swap a joke with sad old geezers.

But when he bought his cigs he'd have a chat,
his week's one conversation, truth to tell,
but time also came and put a stop to that
when old Wattsy got bought out by M. Patel.

And there, 'Time like an ever-rolling stream' 's
what I once trilled behind that boarded front.
A 1000 ages made coal-bearing seams
and even more the hand that sprayed this CUNT

on both Methodist and C of E billboards
once divided in their fight for local souls.
Whichever house more truly was the Lord's
both's pews are filled with cut-price toilet rolls.

Home, home to my woman, never to return
till sexton or survivor has to cram
the bits of clinker scooped out of my urn
down through the rose roots to my dad and mam.

Home, home to my woman, where the fire's lit
these still-chilly mid-May evenings, home to you,
and perished vegetation from the pit
escaping insubstantial up the flue.

Listening to *Lulu*, in our hearth we burn,
as we hear the high Cs rise in stereo,
what was lush swamp club moss and tree fern
at least 300 million years ago.

Shilbottle cobbles, Alban Berg high D
lifted from a source that bears your name,
the one we hear decay, the one we see,
the fern from the foetid forest, as brief flame.

This world, with far too many people in,
starts on the TV logo as a taw,
then ping-pong, tennis, football; then one spin
to show us all, then shots of the Gulf War.

As the coal with reddish dust cools in the grate
on the late-night national news we see
police v. pickets at a coke plant gate,
old violence and old disunity.

The map that's colour-coded Ulster/Eire's
flashed on again, as almost every night.
Behind a tiny coffin with two bearers
men in masks with arms show off their might.

The day's last images recede to first a glow
and then a ball that shrinks back to blank screen.
Turning to love, and sleep's oblivion, I know
what the UNITED that the skin sprayed *has* to mean.

Hanging my clothes up, from my parka hood
may and apple petals, brown and creased,
fall onto the carpet and bring back the flood
of feelings their first falling had released.

I hear like ghosts from all Leeds matches humming
with one concerted voice the bride, the bride
I feel united to, *my* bride is coming
into the bedroom, naked, to my side.

The ones we choose to love become our anchor
when the hawser of the blood tie's hacked or frays.
But a voice that scorns chorales is yelling: *Wanker!*
It's the aerosoling skin I met today's.

My alter ego wouldn't want to know it,
his aerosol vocab would balk at LOVE,
the skin's UNITED underwrites the poet,
the measures carved below the ones above.

I doubt if 30 years of bleak Leeds weather
and 30 falls of apple and of may
will erode the UNITED binding us together.
And now it's your decision. Does it stay?

Next millennium you'll have to search quite hard
to find out where I'm buried, but I'm near
the grave of haberdasher Appleyard,
the pile of HARPs, or some new neoned beer.

Find Byron, Wordsworth, or turn left between
one grave marked Broadbent, one marked Richardson.
Bring some solution with you that can clean
whatever new crude words have been sprayed on.

If love of art, or love, gives you affront
that the grave I'm in 's graffitied, then, maybe,
erase the more offensive FUCK and CUNT
but leave, with the worn UNITED, one small *v*.

victory? For vast, slow, coal-creating forces
that hew the body's seams to get the soul.
Will earth run out of her 'diurnal courses'
before repeating her creation of black coal?

But choose a day like I chose in mid-May
or earlier when apple and hawthorn tree,
no matter if boys boot their ball all day,
cling to their blossoms and won't shake them free—

if, having come this far, somebody reads
these verses, and he/she wants to understand,
face this grave on Beeston Hill, your back to Leeds,
and read the chiselled epitaph I've planned:

Beneath your feet's a poet, then a pit.
Poetry supporter, if you're here to find
how poems can grow from (beat you to it!) SHIT
find the beef, the beer, the bread, then look behind.

Painkillers

I.

My father haunts me in the old men that I find
holding the shop queues up by being slow.
It's always a man like him that I'm behind
just when I thought the pain of him would go
reminding me perhaps it never goes,
with his pension book kept utterly pristine
in a plastic wrapper labelled *Pantyhose*
as if they wouldn't pay if it weren't clean,

or learning to shop so late in his old age
and counting his money slowly from a purse
I'd say from its ornate clasp and shade of beige
was his dead wife's glasses case. I curse,
but silently, secreting pain, at this delay,
the acid in my gut caused by Dad's ghost—
I've got aerogrammes to buy. My love's away!
And the proofs of *Painkillers* to post.

II.

Going for pills to ease the pain I get
from the Post Office on Pension Day,
the chemist's also gives me cause to fret
at more of my dad's ghosts, and more delay
as they queue for their prescriptions without hope
and go looking for the old cures on the shelves,
stumbling into pyramids of scented soap
they once called sissy when they felt 'themselves.'

There are more than in the Post Office in Boots
and I try to pass the time behind such men
by working out the Latin and Greek roots
of cures, the *san-* that's in *Sanatogen*
compounds derived from *derm-* for teenage spots,
suntan creams and lotions prefixed *sol-*
while a double of my dad takes three wild shots
at pronouncing PARACETAMOL.

Changing at York

A directory that runs from B to V,
the Yellow Pages' entries for HOTELS
and TAXIS torn out, the smell of dossers' pee,
saliva in the mouthpiece, whisky smells—
I remember, now that I have to phone,
squashing a *Daily Mail* half full of chips,
to tell the son I left at home alone
my train's delayed, and get cut off by the pips,
how, phoning his mother, late, a little pissed,
changing at York, from some place where I'd read,
I used 2p to lie about the train I'd missed
and ten more to talk my way to some girl's bed
and, in this same kiosk with the stale, sour breath
of queuing callers, drunk, cajoling, lying,
consoling his grandpa for his granny's death,
how I heard him, for the first time ever, crying.

The Act

for Michael Longley & James Simmons

Newcastle Airport and scarcely 7 a.m.
yet they foot the white line out towards the plane
still reeling (or as if) from last night's FED
or macho marathons in someone's bed.
They scorn the breakfast croissants and drink beer,
and who am I to censure or condemn?
I know oblivion's a balm for man's poor brain
and once roistered in male packs as bad as them.
These brews stoke their bravado, numb their fear
but anaesthetize all joy along with pain.

To show they had a weekend cunt or two
they walk as if they'd shagged the whole world stiff.
The squaddies' favourite and much-bandied words
for describing what they'd done on leave to birds
as if it were pub-brawl or DIY
seem to be, I quote, 'bang,' 'bash,' or 'screw,'
if they did anything (a biggish if!)
more than the banter boomed now at the crew
as our plane levels off in a blue sky
along with half-scared cracks on catching syph.

They've lit Full Strengths on DA 141
despite NO SMOKING signs and cabin crew's
polite requests; they want to disobey
because they bow to orders every day.
The soldiers travel pretty light and free
as if they left Newcastle for the sun,
in winter with bare arms that show tattoos.
The stewardesses clearly hate this run,
the squaddies' continuous crude repartee
and constant button-pushing for more booze.

I've heard the same crude words and smutty cracks
and seen the same lads on excursion trains
going back via ferry from Stranraer
queuing at breakfast at the BR bar,
cleaning it out of *Tartan* and *Brown Ale*.
With numbered kitbags piled on luggage racks
just after breakfast bombed out of their brains,
they balance their empty cans in wobbly stacks.
An old woman, with indulgence for things male,
smiles at them and says: 'They're nobbut wains!'

Kids, mostly cocky Geordies and rough Jocks
with voices coming straight out of their boots,
the voices heard in newsreels about coal
or dockers newly dumped onto the dole
after which the army's the next stop.
One who's breakfasted on *Brown Ale* cocks
a nail-bitten, nicotined right thumb, and shoots
with loud saliva salvos a red fox
parting the clean green blades of some new crop
planted by farm families with old roots.

A card! The stewardesses almost throw it
into our laps not wanting to come near
to groping soldiers. We write each fact
we're required to enter by 'The Act':
profession; place of birth; purpose of visit.
The rowdy squaddy, though he doesn't know it
(and if he did he'd brand the freak as 'queer')
is sitting next to one who enters 'poet'
where he puts 'Forces.' But what is it?
My purpose? His? *What* are we doing here?

Being a photographer seems bad enough.
God knows the catcalls that a poet would get!
Newcastle-bound for leave the soldiers rag
the press photographer about his bag
and call him Gert or Daisy, and all laugh.
They shout at him in accents they'd dub 'pouf'
Yoo hoo, hinny! Like your handbag, pet!
Though what he's snapped has made him just as tough
and his handbag hardware could well photograph
these laughing features when they're cold and set.

I don't like the thought of these lads manning blocks
but saw them as you drove me to my flight,
now khakied up, not kaylied but alert,
their minds on something else than Scotch or skirt,
their elbows bending now to cradle guns.
The road's through deep green fields and wheeling flocks
of lapwings soaring, not the sort of sight
the sentry looks for in his narrow box.
'Cursed be dullards whom no cannon stuns'
I quote. They won't read what we three write.

They occupy NO SMOKING seats and smoke,
commandos free a few days from command
which cries for license and I watch them cram
anything boozable, *Brown Ale* to *Babycham*
into their hardened innards, and they drain
whisky/lemonade, *Bacardi/Coke*,
double after double, one in either hand,
boys' drinks spirit-spiked for the real *bloke*!
Neither passengers nor cabin crew complain
as the squaddies keep on smoking as we land.

And as the morning Belfast plane descends
on Newcastle and one soldier looks,
with tears, on what he greets as 'Geordie grass'
and rakes the airport terrace for 'wor lass'
and another hollers to his noisy mates
he's going to have before their short leave ends
'firkins of fucking FED, fantastic fucks!'
I wish for you, my Ulster poet friends,
pleasures with no rough strife, no iron gates,
and letter boxes wide enough for books.

Y

I'm good with curtains
—MRS. THATCHER

The thing I drink
from above the earth
's by *Technoplastics Inc.*
(Fort Worth)

I hear the chinks
of pukka glass
from what I think's
called Business Class,

my taste buds impressed
as bustle helps waft
the Premium repast
to the Y class aft.

Farther fore there's china
and choices for dinner.
The wines get finer,
the glass thinner.

Veuve Cliquot for the man
with a 1st thirst; for me
a tiny ring-pull can
of California Chablis!

From our plastic drinking,
O Ys of all nations,
it's maybe worth thinking
that the one consolation's:

if the engines fail
and we go into a dive
only Ys in the tail
ever seem to survive!

As the stewardesses serve
first to 1st, last to Y,
I can't fail to observe,
as on earth so in the sky,

that the U.S.A.
draws no drapes—
the First Class can pay
while the Y Class gapes—

pour encourager . . .
any man can fly
Premium if he can pay
(or his company).

We curtain the classes
while they eat,
the plastics from glasses,
we are so discreet!

And from LHR to JFK
from JFK to LHR
things are going to stay
just as they are.

Summoned by Bells

The art of letters will come to an end before A.D. 2000 . . .
I shall survive as a curiosity.
—EZRA POUND

O Zeppelins! O Zeppelins!
prayed poet E.P.
any Boche gets 60 pence
to bust this campanolatry!

Doubles, triples, caters, cinques
for corpse or Christmas joys
for him, or anyone who thinks,
may be 'foul nuisance' and mere noise.

Carillons can interfere
and ruin concentration.
I've had it wrecked, my rhythmic ear,
by the new faith of the nation.

So sympathise with E.P.'s plight.
This moment now it's hard to hold
this rhythm in my head and write
while those bloody bells are tolled.

St. Mary Abbot's, they're passé.
What gets into my skull
any time of night and day
are the new bells of John Bull,

The new calls to the nation:
Securi-curi-curi-cor!
Join the fight against inflation!
Double-Chubb your door!

'Beat Inflation' adverts call.
Invest in stronger locks!
Display for all on your front wall
the crime-deterrent box.

Almost every day one goes
and the new faith that it rings
is vested in new videos
and the sacredness of things.

I got done once. No piercing peal
alerted neighbourhood or force
but then there's nothing here to steal
bar 'a few battered books,' of course.

The poor sneak thief, all he could do
he had so little time to act,
was grab a meagre coin or two
and my bag there ready packed.

What bothers me perhaps the most
is I never heard the thief,
being obsessively engrossed
in rhymes of social grief.

In haste behind the garden wall
he unzipped my bag. Bad luck!
One glance told him that his haul
was 50 copies of one book!

Poems! Poems! All by me!
He dropped the lot and ran
(and who would buy hot poetry
from a poor illiterate man?)

deeply pissed by what he'd found,
dumped books and bag unzipped.
He'd've even ditched an Ezra Pound
Cantos manuscript.

I got my books, he went scot-free,
no summons, gaol or fines.
I used him for such poetry
this alarm leaves in these lines

on 'a botched civilisation'
E.P. helped to rebotch
where bells toll for a nation
that's one great Neighbourhood Watch.

Sonnets for August 1945

1. The Morning After

I.

The fire left to itself might smoulder weeks.
Phone cables melt. Paint peels from off back gates.
Kitchen windows crack; the whole street reeks
of horsehair blazing. Still it celebrates.

Though people weep, their tears dry from the heat.
Faces flush with flame, beer, sheer relief
and such a sense of celebration in our street
for me it still means joy though banked with grief.

And that, now clouded, sense of public joy
with war-worn adults wild in their loud fling
has never come again since as a boy
I saw Leeds people dance and heard them sing.

There's still that dark, scorched circle on the road.
The morning after kids like me helped spray
hissing upholstery spring wire that still glowed
and cobbles boiling with black gas tar for VJ.

II.

The Rising Sun was blackened on those flames.
The jabbering tongues of fire consumed its rays.
Hiroshima, Nagasaki were mere names
for us small boys who gloried in our blaze.

The blood-red ball, first burnt to blackout shreds,
took hovering batwing on the bonfire's heat
above the *Rule Britannias* and the bobbing heads
of the VJ hokey-cokey in our street.

The kitchen blackout cloth became a cloak
for me to play at fiend Count Dracula in.
I swirled it near the fire. It filled with smoke.
Heinz ketchup dribbled down my vampire's chin.

That circle of scorched cobbles scarred with tar's
a night-sky globe nerve-rackingly all black,
both hemispheres entire but with no stars,
an Archerless zilch, a Scaleless zodiac.

2. Old Soldiers

Last years of Empire and the fifth of War
and *Camp* coffee extract on the kitchen table.
The Sikh that served the officer I saw
on the label in the label in the label
continuously cloned beyond my eyes,
beyond the range of any human staring,
down to amoeba, atom, neutron size,
but the turbaned bearer never lost his bearing
and nothing shook the bottle off his tray.
Through all infinity and down to almost zero
he holds out and can't die or fade away
loyal to the breakfasting Scots hero.

But since those two high summer days
the U.S. dropped the World's first A-bombs on,
from that child's forever what returns my gaze
is a last chuprassie with all essence gone.

3. The Figure

In each of our Blackpool photos from those years
and, I'll bet, in every family's South Pier snap,
behind the couples with their children on the pier, 's
the same figure standing in frayed suit and cap.

We'd come to plunge regardless in the sea,
ball-shrivellingly chill, but subs all gone,
gorge Mrs. Moore's Full Board, now ration-free,
glad when *I-Speak-Your-Weight* showed pounds put on.

The first snap that I have's from '45.
I've never seen a family group so glad
of its brief freedom, so glad to be alive,
no camera would have caught them looking sad.

He's there, in the same frayed suit, in '51,
that figure in each photo at the back
who sent us all sauntering towards the sun
and the tripod, and the biped draped in black.

4. Black & White

If we had the cameras then we've got today
since Oblivion, always deep, grew even deeper
the moment of the flash that made VJ
and the boom made almost pro ones so much cheaper,
I'd have snaps of me happy and pre-teen
in pale, affordable Fuji for the part
of innocence that never could have been
born just in time to see the World War start.

The ugly ducklings changed to sitting ducks!

Now everything gets clicked at the loud clock
the shots and shutters sound like 's Captain Hook's
ticking implacably inside the croc.

If he wants his shadow back the Peter Pan
who cowers since Hiroshima in us all
will have to keep returning to Japan
till the blast-cast shape walks with him off the wall.

5. Snap

Uncle Wilf in khaki but decapitated,
and he'd survived the jungle and the Japs,
so his grin's gone when we all celebrated
Hirohito's empire in collapse.

My shorter father's all in and looks glad
and full of euphoria he'd never found
before, or since, and I'm with the grocer's lad
two fingers turned the positive way round!

Innocence, that fraying Kirby wire
that briefly held the whole weight of the nation
over the common element of fire
that bonded the A-bomb blast to celebration,
our VJ bonfire to Jehovahspeak,
the hotline Jesus got instructions from,
and, at Pentecost, Apostles their technique
of saying in every language: *Ban the Bomb!*

6. First Aid in English

First Aid in English, my first grammar book
with a cross on the light blue cover of dark blue
drilled into a [?] of parrots that one rook
became a congregation when it's two.

We chanted gaggle, bevy, coven, herd
between the Nazi and the Japanese defeat.
Did even the dodo couple have its word
that became, in the last one's lifetime, obsolete?

Collective nouns but mostly bird or beast.
Ghetto and gulag weren't quite current then.
The fauna of our infancies decreased
as new nouns grew collectivising men.

Cats in their clowder, lions in their pride,
but there's no aid in English, first or last,
for a [Fill in the Blank] of genocide
or more than one [Please Tick] atomic blast.

7. The Birds of Japan

Campi Phlegraei, Lake Nyos of Wum,
their sulphur could asphyxiate whole flocks
but combustibility had not yet come
to the femto-seconds of the *Fiat Nox*:
men made magma, flesh made fumaroles,
first mottled by the flash to brief mofettes
and Hiroshima's fast pressurising souls
hissed through the fissures in mephitic jets.

Did the birds burst into song as they ignited
above billowing waves of cloud up in the sky,
hosannahs too short-lived to have alighted
on a Bomb-Age Basho, or a Hokusai?

Apostles of that pinioned Pentecost
of chirrupings cremated on the wing
will have to talk their ghosts down, or we're lost.
Until we know what they sang, who can sing?

The Pomegranates of Patmos

We may be that generation that sees Armageddon.
—RONALD REAGAN, 1980

My brother, my bright twin, Prochorus,
I think his bright future's been wrecked.
When we've both got our lives before us
he's gone and joined this weird sect.

He sits in a cave with his guru,
a batty old bugger called John,
and scribbles on scrolls stuff to scare you
while the rabbi goes rabbiting on.

He seems dead to us, does my brother.
He's been so thoroughly brainwashed by John.
'I look in your eyes,' said our mother,
'but the bright boy behind them has gone.'

And the God with gargantuan ΓΡΑΨΟΝ
commanding that crackpot to write
is a Big Daddy bastard who craps on
the Garden of Earthly Delight.

If that sect's idea of a Maker's
one who'll rid the world of the sea
I'm sitting beside watching breakers
he's the wrong bloody maker for me.

Who believes that their God began it
when he's ready to end it so soon,
the splendours of Patmos, the planet,
and the sea and the stars and the moon?

There'll always be people who'll welcome
the end of the sea and the sky
and wail to their God to make Hell come
and rejoice to hear the damned cry,

a date ringed in red in their diary
when they know that Doomsday will be
sure they'll be safe from the fiery
Gehenna engulfing, among billions, me!

I tell him it's crap, his Apocalypse.
I'm happy here in this world as I am.
I'd sooner wear shorts specked with fig pips
than get all togaed up for the Lamb.

If begged to go up where their Lamb is,
those skyscrapers of chrysolite,
kitted out in a cloud-issue chlamys,
with no darkness, then give me the night,

night with its passion and peril,
Patmos with pomegranates and figs
not towerblocks built out of beryl
and glazed with best sardonyx.

When Prochorus comes back from a session
up the hill in the cave with the saint,
he plunges me straight into depression
and, more than once, has made mother feel faint.

All he sees is immediately made
an emblem, a symbol, a fable,
the visible world a mere preaching aid,
even the food mother lays on the table.

An Apocalyptic cock on his heap,
Prochorus crowed as I tried to dine:
'Awake, ye drunkards, and weep,
and howl, all ye drinkers of wine!'

In one of his scrolls envisioning Hell
where the divine allowed him to delve,
in Joel, son of Pethuel
(he added, the pedant, I. 12!),

he found a quotation that made his day
and he tried to use to mar mine,
how pomegranates would wither away
and shrivelled grapes hang from the vine.

He tried to convince me but didn't succeed,
as I spiked out the vermilion gel
from the pomegranate, that its seed
stood for the sperm of the Future flame-lit from Hell,

an orb of embryos still to be born,
a globe of sperm globules that redden
not with the glow of the Aegean dawn
but the fires of his God's Armageddon.

My orb of nibbleable rubies
packed deliciously side by side
his roes of doom-destined babies
carmine with God's cosmocide.

The pomegranate! If forced to compare,
to claim back what eschatology stole,
what about, once you've licked back the hair,
the glossed moistness of a girl's hole?

He could take a gem-packed pomegranate,
best subjected to kisses and suction,
and somehow make it stand for the planet
destined for fiery destruction.

But in Kadesh in the deserts of Zin,
I asserted, the children of Israel chode
their leader Moses for dumping them in
what they called an *evil* abode.

They called that place evil, and why?
(Ask your divine, he should know!)
Because the deserts of Zin were dry
so that no pomegranates could grow.

They saw no hope of staying alive
without the fruits you'd love to see blighted
(see NUMBERS XX. 5—
not bad for one branded 'benighted'!)

Prochorus wasn't prepared for debate.
He and his sort preferred
pouring out endless sermons of hate
and from us not a dicky bird.

The more he went on about how our isle
would vanish along with its ocean
the more I spat kernels and flashed him a smile
and ate more in provoking slow motion.

And what made my brother really rave
and hiccup and spit 666,
what finally sent him back to his cave
were my suckings and sensual licks.

Each seed I impaled I'd hold up high
as though appraising a turquoise,
then with a satisfied sensual sigh
suck off the gel with a loud noise.

Apoplectic with Apocalypse,
his eyes popped watching me chew,
he frothed at the mouth as I smacked my lips
at the bliss of each nibbled red bijou.

So that verse (Rev. XXII.2)
about the fruit tree with 12 different crops
was my brother's addition, if John only knew,
as a revenge for me smacking my chops.

But I knew that I'd never be beaten
by his brayings of blast and of blaze,
and since then, when disheartened, I've eaten
pomegranates to give joy to my days.

And their flowers also are so brave and red,
a redness I've seen intensify
when the storm pressed down and overhead
the darkest clouds massed in the sky.

When the storm clouds bear down their most black,
at the moment the gloom looms most low,
the blown bright balausts bugle back
their chromatic jubilo.

The Doomsday Clock's set at 5 to.
The lovers I follow have time for their stroll
and to let their sensual selves come alive to
the Patmos that gladdens the soul,

the Patmos of figs and pomegranates,
the Patmos of the sea and the shore,
Patmos on earth among planets,
Patmos that's Patmos and no metaphor.

I'm so weary of all metaphorers.
From now on my most pressing ambition's
to debrainwash all like Prochorus
made Moonies by metaphysicians.

But my poor brother could never respond.
I couldn't undermine his defences.
His brain went before him to the Beyond.
He took all leave of his senses.

My brother's heart was turned to stone.
So my revenge on St. John's to instil
in lovers like these, who think they're alone,
the joy John and his ilk want to kill,

and try any charm or trick
to help frightened humans affirm
small moments against the rhetoric
of St. Cosmocankerworm.

And I follow them lovingly strolling
by the sea I was always beside
with the breakers that I watched still rolling
though it's 2,000 years since I died.

Though the rubbish that's out there floating
shows these days are far distant from mine,
no one should rush into quoting
St. John the Doomsday Divine.

Some can't resist the temptation to preach
"The End of the World Is Nigh"
when they see the shit on the beach
or white dishes scanning the sky.

And the johnnies jostling for sea room
like the eelskins of very sick eels
Prochorus would see as new signs of doom
and the angels halfway through the seals.

My charms are mere whispers in lovers' ears
against the loud St. End-It-All
and Prochorus would say my present career's
like the Serpent's before the Fall.

I know nipples brushed by fingertips
that mole up out of their mound
may not arrest their Apocalypse
but it brings the senses to ground.

Lover and lover, a man and his wife,
so grounded assert the sheer
absolute thisness of sublunar life
and not the hereafter, the *here*.

And maybe senses so grounded
will not always be straining to hear
the moment the trumpets are sounded
when the end of the world is near.

And so subliminally into their Sony
I'll put words that I've long thought obscene,
a dose of that dismal old Johnny
but more as a *Weltschmerz* vaccine,

a charm against all Holocausters
and the Patmos Apocalypse freak
and give them the joys that life fosters—
they go back to work in a week!

I follow them walking arm in brown arm.
I sit near to them in the taverna
whispering pagan words as a charm
against the blight of this isle's World-Burner.

By the beach that's a little bit shitty
what I'll sow in these lovers' brains
is a pop poemegranatey ditty
with six verses but *seven* refrains:

1-2-3-4-
5-6-7
their silvery fire
is staying in Heaven.

Seven seals, love,
and it's said they're at six.
We're lucky to live
with starlight and sex.

1-2-3-4-
5-6-7
their silvery fire
is staying in Heaven.

The stars shine. The moon wanes.
Your left hand undoes
my 501s.
I count the Pleiades.

1-2-3-4-
5-6-7
their silvery fire
is staying in Heaven.

To hell with St. John's
life-loathing vision
when I feel in my jeans
your fingers go fishing.

1-2-3-4-
5-6-7
their silvery fire
is staying in Heaven.

Your turn to count.
My turn to lick
your moistening cunt
like a fig, fig.

1-2-3-4-
5-6-7
their silvery fire
is staying in Heaven.

No stars are falling,
all the figs ripen.
I have a gut feeling
the World's End won't happen.

1-2-3-4-
5-6-7
their silvery fire
is staying in Heaven.

The stars won't fall
nor will the fig.
Our hearts are so full
as we fuck, fuck.

1-2-3-4-
5-6-7
their silvery fire
is staying in Heaven.

American Poems

The Fire Gap

A poem with two tails

The fire patrol plane's tail fins flash.
I see it suddenly swoop low,
or maybe it's scouting out the hash
some crackers round here grow.
There's nothing on our land to hide,
no marijuana here,
I think the patrol's quite satisfied
the fire gap's bulldozed clear.
I'm not concerned what's in the air
but what's beneath my feet.
This fire gap I walk on's where
the snake and I will meet.
Where we live is much the same
as other land in the U.S.,
half kept cultivated, tame,
and half left wilderness,
and living on this fire gap
between wilderness and tilled
is the snake my neighbours want to trap;
they want 'the motherfucker' killed.
One man I know round here who's mean
would blast the hole with dynamite
or flood the lair with gasoline
and maybe set the woods alight.
Against all truculent advice
I've let the rattler stay,
and go each day with my flask of ice
to my writing shed this way.

I think the land's quite big enough
to contain both him and me
as long as the odd, discarded slough
is all of the snake I see.
But I'm aware that one day on this track
there'll be, when I'm least alert,
all six feet of diamondback
poised to do me mortal hurt,
or I might find its shrugged-off shed,
'clothes on the beach,' 'gone missing,'
and just when I supposed him dead
he's right behind me, hissing.
Although I know I risk my neck
each time I pass, I stare
into the gopher hole to check
for signs the rattler's there.
I see the gopher's pile of dirt
with like rope marks dragged through
and I'm at once on the alert
for the killer of the two.
Is it perverse of me to start
each morning as I pass the hole
with a sudden pounding of my heart,
my fear out of control,
my Adam's apple in a vice
so scared that I mistake
the rattle of my thermos ice
for the angry rattlesnake?
I've started when a pine twig broke
or found I'd only been afraid
of some broken branch of dead live oak
zigzagged with sun and shade.
But if some barley starts to sway
against the movement of the breeze

and most blades lean the other way
that's when you'd better freeze.
If you've dragged a garden hose
through grass that's one foot tall
that's the way the rattler goes
if you catch a glimpse at all.
I killed snakes once, about a score
in Africa and in Brazil
yet they filled me with such awe
it seemed gross sacrilege to kill.
Once with matchet and domestic broom
I duelled with a hooded snake
with frightened children in the room
and all our lives at stake.
The snake and I swayed to and fro.
I swung the broom. Her thick hood spread.
I jabbed the broom. She rode the blow
and I hacked off her hooded head.
Then I lopped this 'laithly worm'
and sliced the creature into nine
reptilian lengths that I saw squirm
as if still one connected spine.
The gaps between the bits I'd lopped
seemed supple snake though made of air
so that I wondered where life stopped
and if death started, where?
Since that time I've never killed
any snake that's come my way
between the wild land and the tilled
where I walk every day
towards my woodland writing shed,
my heart mysteriously stirred
if I get a glimpse of tail or head
or think its rattle's what I heard

when it's only a cicada's chirr
that grates on my cocked ear
not the hidden it/him/her
it so scares me to hear.
I've tried at last to come to terms
and deal only through my craft
with this laithliest of laithly worms
with poison fore, grim music aft,
that makes my heart jam up my throat
and fills me with fear and wonder
as at the sound made when *Der Tod*
(in Strasbourg) *schlägt die Stunde*.
The sainted heroes of the Church
beheaded serpents who stood for
the Mother whose name they had to smirch
to get their own foot in the door.
We had to fight you to survive:
Darkness versus Light!
Now I want you on my land alive
and I don't want to fight.
Smitten by Jehovah's curses:
On thy belly thou must go!
I don't think Light is what you're versus,
though the Bible tells me so.
I've seen you basking in the sun.
I've seen you entering the earth.
Darkness and Light to you are one.
You link together death and birth.
The Bible has another fable
that almost puts us on a par,
how God smote low ambitious Babel
for trying to reach too far.
From being once your mortal foe
and wanting all your kind to die

because the Bible told me so,
I now almost identify.
So, snake, old rhyming slang's
equivalent for looking glass,
when I walk here draw back your fangs
and let your unlikely ally pass.
I'm walking to my shed to write
and work out how they're linked
what's called the Darkness and the Light
before we all become extinct.
Laithly, maybe, but Earth-lover,
unmolested, let me go.
so my struggles might discover
what you already know.
As the low-flying fire patrol
makes the slash and live oaks sway
I go past the deep-dug gopher hole
where I hope my snake will stay
and stay forever if it likes.
I swear no one on this land will kill
the rattlesnake unless it strikes;
then, I give my word, I will.
This fire gap we trim with care
and mow short twice a year
is where we sometimes spot a hare,
a polecat, snake, or deer.
They're off so fast one scarcely sees
retreating scut or tail
before they're lost among the trees
and they've thrown you off their trail.
But there's one who doesn't make
quick dashes for the undergrowth
nor bolts for the barley—that's the snake
whose length can bridge them both.

I've seen it span the fire gap,
its whole six feet stretched out,
the wild touched by its rattle tip,
the tilled field by its snout.
Stretched out where the scrub's been mown
the rattler's lordly manner
treats the earth as all its own,
gap, cereals, savannah.
Best keep to my land if you're wise.
Once you cross my boundary line
the Bible Belters exorcise
all traces of the serpentine,
from Satan plain to demon drink,
the flesh you're blamed for keeping hot,
all earth-embracing snakes that slink
whether poisonous or not,
the fairy, pacifist, the Red,
maybe somebody who loves the Muse—
are all forms of the serpent's head
their God tells them to bruise,

the God invoked in Titusville
on last night's local news
against the enemies they'd kill
with the blessed and baptised Cruise.

I fear they're not the sort to see,
these Christians of the South,
the only real eternity
is a tale (like your tail) in the mou

The Heartless Art

In memoriam
S.T. died April 4, 1985

Death is in your house, but I'm out here
sackclothing kumquats against the forecast freeze,
filling the hole you took two days to clear
of briars, beer cans, and bleached, barkless trees,
with hackberry leaves, pine needles, stuff like that.
Next spring, when you're no longer here,
we'll have the land grassed over and quite flat.

When the southern sun starts setting it sets fast.
I've time to tip one more load if I run.
Because I know this light could be your last
I drain the day of every drop of sun.
The barrow wheel spins round with a clock's tick.
I hear, three fields away, a hunter's gun,
you, in the silence after, being sick.

I watched you, very weak, negotiate
the childproof pill jar, panting to draw breath,
and when you managed it you poured your hate
more on the poured-out contents than on death,
and, like Baptists uttering Beelzebub
syllable by syllable, spat Meth-
a-done, and there's also the poetic rub!

I've often heard my fellow poets (or those
who write in metres something like my own
with rhyme and rhythm, not in chopped-up prose,
and brood on man's mortality) bemoan
the insufficiency of rhymes for death—
hence my syllabifying Methadone
instead of just saying that you fought for breath.

Maybe the main but not the only cause;
a piece of engineering I'll explain.
Each syllable was followed by a pause
for breathlessness, and scorn of drugs for pain.
Another reason, though, was to delay
the use of one more rhyme stored in my brain
that, alas, I'll have a use for any day.

I'd stored away this rhyme when we first met.
Knowing you crawled on hands and knees to prime
our water pump, I'll expiate one debt
by finally revealing that stored rhyme
that has the same relentlessness as death
and comes to every one of us in time
and comes to you this April full moon, SETH!

In return for all those oily working parts
you took the time and trouble to explain,
the pump that coughs, the saw that never starts,
I'll show you to distract you from the pain
you feel, except when napping, all the time
because you won't take drugs that dull the brain,
a bit about my metre, line, and rhyme.

In Arthur Symons' *St. Teresa,* Nazaréth
is stressed on the last against its spoken flow
to engineer the contrast Jesus/Death.
Do I endorse that contrast? I don't, no!
To have a life on earth and then want Heaven
seems like that all-night bar sign down below
that says that Happy Hour's from 4 to 7.

Package lounges are like ambulances:
the bourbon-bibber stares at us and glowers
at what he thinks are pained or pitying glances.
We don't see his face but he sees ours.
The non-dying don't see you but you see them
passing by to other rooms with flowers
as you fill the shining kidney with red phlegm.

I've left some spaces (   )[1]
benumbed by morphia and Methadone
until the (   )[2] of April, (   )[3]
When I began these lines could I have known
that the nurse's registration of the time
you let your spirit go with one last groan
would help complete the first- and third-line rhyme?

Those bits I added later. Them apart
I wrote this *in memoriam* for Seth,
meant to show him something of my art,
almost a whole week before his death.
The last thing the dying want to read,
I thought, 's a poem, and didn't show it,
and you, not dying yet, why should you need
to know the final failure of the poet?

[1] how you stayed alive   /   [2] 4th   /   [3] 10:05

Broadway

A flop is when the star's first-night bouquets outlast the show itself by several days.

Following Pine

I.

When a plumber glues some lengths of PVC
that pipe our cold spring water from its source,
or a carpenter fits porch posts, and they see,
from below or from above, the heartwood floors
made from virgin lumber, such men say,
as if they'd taught each other the same line:
Boards like them boards don't exist today!
then maybe add: *Now everything's new pine.*

Though the house is in a scant surviving wood
that has black walnut, hackberry, pecan,
and moss-festooned live oaks that have withstood
centuries more of bad news than a man,
sometimes we can drive an hour or more
and see nothing but dense pine trees on both sides
and no glimpse of the timbers for such floors
from virgin forest laid for virgin brides.

The feller/buncher and de-limber groans,
grappling the grovelling pines, and dozing flat
a whole stand to a mess of stumps and stones
like some Goliath gorged on them, then shat
what was no use to him back on the land.
The sun and moon are sharing the same sky
as we drive by this totally depleted stand
marked down for GP planks and layer-peeled ply.

We'd set off early but shrill loggers' saws
were already shrieking in the stands of pines.
Fresh-felled, lopped slash pine tree trunks in their scores
were being bulldozed into ordered lines
waiting for the trucks in long convoy.
The trimmed-off branches were already burning.
The quiet, early road we'd wanted to enjoy
we did, but met the timber trucks returning.

Our early start was so that we could get
the trees we'd gone to buy into the ground,
watered and well mulched, before sunset,
and not be digging in the dark with snakes around.
So with fig trees, vines, and apples in the back,
wilting and losing their Tree Garden sheen,
we see on the road ahead a sky half black
and half as brilliantly blue as it had been.

The fast track was all wet, the crawler lane
we'd driven in most of the morning, dry.
The west side was in sun, the east in rain.
The east had black, the west had bright blue sky.
Armadillo blood, on the one side, 's washed away
and, on the other, farther on, sun-dried,
according as the car-crushed creature lay
on the highway's wet or sunny side.

Killed by traffic flowing through the night,
armadillos, rats, snake, dog, raccoon,
dead on both road verges, left and right,
are scavenged on and half decayed by noon,
and browsed over with hummed hubbub by blowfly
like loud necklaces, beads gone berserk,
that, whatever the day's weather, wet or dry,
stay a high gloss green and do their work.

And as we accelerated fast and overtook,
moving on the rain side as we did,
first one and then another timber truck,
the sudden wet road made me scared we'd skid.
My heart leaped instantly into my mouth
till we seemed safe between two loads of pine,
part of the convoy travelling due south
with east lane raining and west side fine.

Was it the danger that made me hold my breath,
the quick injection of adrenalin,
the vision of our simultaneous death
and the crushed Toyota we were riding in,
or the giant raindrops that were pelting
onto the windshield and shot through with sun,
that made it seem the two of us were melting
and in a radiant decay becoming one?

Good job with such visions going on
that you were driving and you kept your head,
or that sense of fleshly glory would be gone
with the visionary who sensed it, and you, dead,
as dead as the armadillo, possum or raccoon
killed by the nighttime traffic and well
advanced into decay by afternoon
and already giving off a putrid smell.

At least the storm cleaned love bugs off the car
and washed the windscreen glass so you could drive.
When they copulate in swarms you can't see far.
They'd sooner fuck their brains out than survive.
They hit the car, embracing, and, squashed flat,
their twinned remains are merged into one mess.
It is just the crushed canoodling gnat
that needs for its Nirvana nothingness?

Flattened in airborne couples as they fucked,
their squashed millions would make the windscreen dark
if the wipers didn't constantly conduct
the dead to sectors round the dozed-clear arc.
Choked radiators, speckled bumper bars
spattered with love bugs, two by two,
camouflage the colour of parked cars
pulled up at *Chang's Mongolian Barbecue.*

From then on we were well and truly stuck
and anxious to get back to plant our trees
behind the huge pine-loaded lumber truck,
its red flag flapping in the slipstream breeze.
Because the lashed lopped slash was newly cut
the pungency of pine filled all the air.
We have to drive with all our windows shut,
the smell of pine too powerful to bear.

Now quite impossible to overtake,
the convoy crawls up Highway 26.
Your foot keeps hovering above the brake
behind future coffin lids and cocktail sticks.
Our impatience at the slowness of the road
was not repugnance at the smell of pine,
however pungent, but worry for our load
of apple, pear, and fig, and muscadine.

Pine's the lingering perfume newlyweds
in just-built houses smell off panelling,
off squeaky floorboards, off their platform beds,
that cows smell when their rheumy nostrils sting
and tingle on electric pasture fences,
of the U.S.A.'s best-selling bathroom spray
spritzed against those stinks that shock the senses,
shit, decomposition, and decay.

This is the smell in Walden that Thoreau's
cabin builder's hands gave to his lunch,
the resinous pitch that prickled in his nose
whenever he took a sandwich out to munch,
and, maybe, thinking morosely as he chews
how woodlands mostly end up wooden goods,
the wrapping of his butties, week-old news
was also nature once, and someone's woods.

In some sub-Walden worlds his dream survives
though these dreams of independence are nightmares
where retiree DIYers save their lives
while everyone around them's losing theirs.
Spacemen go one way, these pioneers
mole down into the earth to find a place
to weather out the days, weeks, even years
that may well, but for these, kill off our race.

Considering their years it's maybe kinder
when they burrow in the ground like gophers do
not to offer them the sobering reminder
that rattlesnakes use gopher burrows too.
However layered with rocks and earth the roof,
however stocked with freeze-drieds (praise the Lord!),
however broad the door, how bulletproof,
no matter how much water they have stored,

until the radiation-count all-clear
broadcast (they don't say how) on radio,
when they can, but cautiously, then reappear,
death got there before them, though they grow
by battery-powered Mazda light-bulb beams
alfalfa sprouts, damp blotting pads of cress,
while nations torn apart by common dreams
are united in a state of Nothingness.

Being neither newlyweds nor retirees
today we bought five figs, a pear, a vine,
and still have some belief in planting trees
with lifespans more than three times yours and mine.
Most of my life I've wanted to believe
those words of Luther that I've half endorsed
about planting an apple tree the very eve
of the Apocalypse, or the Holocaust.

Every time my bags of red goat leather
are lying labelled ENGLAND in the hall
and we take our last stroll round the land together
whether it's winter, summer, spring, or fall,
there's always one last job I find to do,
pruned branches that I need to burn,
one last load of needles left to strew—
a way of guaranteeing my return.

A neighbour learns the skills they call 'survival,'
living wild off sabal palm and game
killed by various means, knife, bow, or rifle,
even by throttling; me, I've learned to name
and know the subtle differences between
what once was only 'woods,' or was before
mere nameless leaves of slightly varied green
but is now, say, persimmon or possumhaw.

Who lives for the future, who for now?
What good's the *cigale*'s way, or the *fourmi*'s
if both end up as nothing anyhow
unless they look at life like Socrates
who wished, at the very end, to learn to play
a new air on his novice lyre. *Why?*
said his teacher, *This is your last day.*
To know it before I die was the reply.

II.

Chill, sterile, waterless, inert,
but full, the moon illuminates the night
enough for us to dig the still-warm dirt
and plant the trees we've brought home by its light—
that globe above so different from here,
where no one lives and nothing ever grows,
no soil, no moisture, and no atmosphere
to culture kumquats in or grow a rose.

From that great plain of death, inert and chill,
light may rebound but life will never come.
Those so-called seas are sterile, dry, and still,
Mare Serenitatis, Sinus Iridum.
And yet, I thought, and yet, where would we be
without these light beams bounced off that dead land,
without these ungrassed dunes and lifeless sea
shedding their pallor on my scooping hand?

Light from a surface so cold and so dead
was the one we planted our new fruit trees by,
the one that casts its glow now on our bed,
the one I find reflected in your eye.
Is not extinction with its eerie light
the appropriate presider when one swears
to sustain each other through the world of night
we've both decided is 'best borne in pairs'?

We see all that we need to by a light
beamed off a barrenness of pits and plain,
off the '69 Apollo landing site
where planted flag and giant step remain.
That place, some men aspire to, discovers,
with light reflected from plains pocked with pits,
plant life, a yellow house, a pair of lovers,
uniting in their love deep opposites.

This Earth, and this Earth's sterile satellite
won't always be, like life and death, apart,
if Man's destructive mind with Nature's might
leaves the planet a pitted lunar chart
with no one here to name the barren craters
after rainbows, or discoverers, or peace,
though there'll be peace when Earth's worst agitators
find in final dissolution their release.

Despite barricaded bolt holes deep below
it's often said that what will come off best
once, step by step, we've reached All-Systems-Go,
of all life on this Earth, 's the lowliest:
those bugs tonight like high-roast coffee beans
that fling themselves at flames and self-destruct,
the blue wasp juicing bugs like tangerines,
fat bucking locusts jockeyed on and sucked,

these trawling spiders that have rigged their nets
halfway between our porch lamps and the night,
their dawn webs threaded with dew jewelettes
and hauls of flies caught lurching for our light,
a blundering beetle with black laquered back
that dialled its liquidation to the spider's limb,
embalmed in abseil/bell pull, a stored snack
swathed in white cerements of sticky scrim.

Phoning that zero got the spider quick.
Each leg's in touch with 45 degrees
of laddered circle where the insects stick
on tacky wires their weaver walks with ease.
Even the love bugs, randy and ridiculous,
coupling regardless of death close behind,
could still be fucking after all of us
are merged in the molten mess made of Mankind.

Falling asleep to loud cicada chirrs,
to scuttling cockroach, crashing carapace,
the noises that I hear are our inheritors
who'll know the Earth both B and A our race.
And underneath those floorboards of good heart
I think I hear the slither of a snake
and then the rodent prey the snake makes start.
Let's forget about the world until we wake!

III.

Each board of 'tongue in groove' 's scored by a line
I measure insect movements by from bed.
A spider crossing long-since scentless pine
racks its night catch on a slender thread.
The blowfly's hawsered body still looks wet
though all night it's been suspended in the dry.
It spins round, flashing, in the spider's net
with shredded cockroach wings and antennae.

I knew I'd wake today and find you gone
and look out of the window, knowing where
you'd be so early, still with nothing on,
watering our new plants with drowsy care.
The night, already stripped of half its dark,
now with the rest sloughed off, 's revealed as day,
and the sun already makes small rainbows arc
out of the hose's nozzle drizzling spray.

Crunching the rusty needles that I strew
to stunt the weed growth on the paths we hacked
I come towards you and am naked too,
and, being naked, feel my nerves react
to the pliant give and snap of spider thread,
snagged on a nipple, sliding on my sweat,
pinged on a whisker, snapped against my head—
the night survivor loosened from the net.

Though impossible to hear I sense each ping
as of an instrument too tautly strung
with notes too high for human voice to sing
and, in any case, not heard if ever sung,
and maybe like that air of Socrates,
I hope he played at least once with some skill,
transposed beyond our ken into high keys
I can't hear now, and know I never will.

For all that unseen threads break on my face,
for all these cordons of cobweb caress,
I walk towards you and don't change my pace
feeling each broken thread one stricture less
against my passage to the world of day.
I can only know the last one when it breaks.
You can't see them ahead, and anyway,
I have to scan the ground for rattlesnakes.

I wonder as I walk still half awake
if the trees that baked a bit long in the boot
and we'd planted in the dark would ever take
and if we'd ever taste their longed-for fruit.
I pass what's become in 12 months gut-high pine
planted last summer in a long close row
as our few acres' demarcation line
and I will what's still a hedge to grow less slow,

and be tall enough to mask the present view
of you watering the saplings as you spray
rainbows at fig trees planted 2-1-2
and both of us still nude at break of day.
A morning incense smokes off well-doused ground.
Everywhere you water rainbows shine.
This private haven that we two have found
might be the more so when enclosed with pine.

Trenton, Florida

73

The Mother of the Muses

In memoriam Emmanuel Stratas,
born Crete 1903, died Toronto 1987

After I've lit the fire and looked outside
and found us snowbound and the roads all blocked,
anxious to prove my memory's not ossified
and the way into that storehouse still unlocked,
as it's easier to remember poetry,
I try to remember, but soon find it hard,
a speech from *Prometheus* a boy from Greece B.C.
scratched, to help him learn it, on a shard.

I remember the museum, and I could eke
his scratch marks out, and could complete
the . . . however many lines there were of Greek
and didn't think it then much of a feat.
But now, not that much later, when I find
the verses I once knew beyond recall
I resolve to bring all yesterday to mind,
our visit to your father, each fact, *all.*

Seeing the Home he's in 's made me obsessed
with remembering those verses I once knew
and setting myself this little memory test
I don't think, at the moment, I'll come through.
It's the Memory, Mother of the Muses, bit.
Prometheus, in words I do recall reciting
but can't quote now, and they're so apposite,
claiming he gave Mankind the gift of writing,

along with fire the Gods withheld from men
who'd lived like ants in caves deprived of light
they could well end up living in again
if we let what flesh first roasted on ignite
a Burning of the Books far more extreme
than any screeching Führer could inspire,
the dark side of the proud Promethean dream
our globe enveloped in his gift of fire.

He bequeathed to baker and to bombardier,
to help benighted men develop faster,
two forms of fire, the gentle one in here,
and what the *Luftwaffe* unleashed, *and* the Lancaster.
One beneficial and one baleful form,
the fire I lit a while since in the grate
that's keeping me, as I sit writing, warm
and what gutted Goethestrasse on this date,

beginning yesterday to be precise
and shown on film from forty years ago
in a Home for the Aged almost glazed with ice
and surrounded by obliterating snow.
We had the choice of watching on TV
Dresden destroyed, then watching its rebirth,
or, with the world outside too blizzardful to see,
live, the senile not long for this earth.

Piles of cracked ice tiles where ploughs try to push
the muddied new falls onto shattered slates,
the glittering shrapnel of grey frozen slush,
a blitz debris fresh snow obliterates
along with what was cleared the day before
bringing even the snowploughs to a halt.
And their lives are frozen solid and won't thaw
with no memory to fling its sparks of salt.

The outer world of blur reflects their inner,
these Rest Home denizens who don't quite know
whether they've just had breakfast, lunch, or dinner,
or stare, between three lunches, at the snow.
Long icicles from the low roof meet
the frozen drifts below and block their view
of flurry and blizzard in the snowed-up street
and of a sky that for a month has shown no blue.

Elsie's been her own optometrist,
measuring the daily way her sight declines
into a growing ball of flashing mist.
She trains her failing sight on outside signs:
the church's COME ALIVE IN '85!
the small hand on the *Export A* ad clock,
the flashing neon on the truck-stop dive
pulsing with strobe lights and jukebox rock,

the little red Scottie on the STOOP & SCOOP
but not the cute eye cast towards its rear,
the little rounded pile of heaped red poop
the owners are required to bend and clear.
To imagine herself so stooping is a feat
as hard as that of gymnasts she has seen
lissom in white leotards compete
in trampolining on the TV screen.

There's one with mashed dinner who can't summon
yet again the appetite to smear
the food about the shrunk face of a woman
weeping for death in her 92nd year.
And of the life she lived remembers little
and stares, like someone playing Kim's Game
at the tray beneath her nose that fills with spittle
whose bubbles fill with faces with no name.

Lilian, whose love made her decide
to check in with her mate who'd had a stroke,
lost all her spryness once her husband died . . .
He had a beautiful . . . all made of oak . . .
silk inside . . . brass handles . . . tries to find
alternatives . . . *that long thing where you lie*
for words like coffin that have slipped her mind
and forgetting, not the funeral, makes her cry.

And Anne, who treats her roommates to her 'news'
though every day her news is just the same
how she'd just come back from *such a lovely cruise*
to that famous island . . . I forget its name . . .
Born before the Boer War, me, and so
I'm too old to remember I suppose . . .
then tries again . . . *the island's called . . . you know . . .*
that place, you know . . . where everybody goes . . .

First Gene had one and then a second cane
and then, in weeks, a walker of cold chrome,
now in a wheelchair wails for the Ukraine,
sobbing in soiled pants for what was home.
Is that horror at what's on the TV screen
or just the way the stroke makes Jock's jaw hang?
Though nobody quite knows what his words mean
they hear Scots diphthongs in the New World twang.

And like the Irish Sea on Blackpool Beach,
where Joan was once the pick of bathing belles,
the Lancashire she once had in her speech
seeps into Canadian as she retells
whose legs now ooze out water, who can't walk,
how she was 'champion at tap,' 'the flower'
(she poises the petals on the now frail stalk)
'of the ballet troupe at Blackpool Tower.'

You won't hear Gene, Eugene, Yevgeny speak
to nurses now, or God, in any other tongue
but his Ukrainian, nor your dad Greek,
all that's left to them of being young.
Life comes full circle when we die.
The circumference is finally complete,
so we shouldn't wonder too much why
his speech went back, a stowaway, to Crete.

Dispersal and displacement, willed or not,
from homeland to the room the three share here,
one Ukrainian, one Cretan, and one Scot
grow less Canadian as death draws near.
Jock sees a boozer in a Glasgow street,
and Eugene glittering icons, candles, prayer,
and for your dad a thorn-thick crag in Crete
with oregano and goat smells in the air.

And home? Where is it now? The olive grove
may well be levelled under folds of tar.
The wooden house made joyful with a stove
has gone the way of Tsar and samovar.
The small house with 8 people to a room
with no privacy for quiet thought or sex
bulldozed in the island's tourist boom
to make way for Big Macs and discotheques.

Beribboned hats and bold embroidered sashes
once helped another émigré forget
that Canada was going to get his ashes
and that Estonia's still Soviet.
But now the last of those old-timers
couldn't tell one folk dance from another
and mistakes in the mists of his Alzheimer's
the nurse who wipes his bottom for his mother.

Some hoard memories as some hoard gold
against that rapidly approaching day
that's all they have to live on, being old,
but find their savings spirited away.
What's the point of having lived at all
in the much-snapped duplex in Etobicoke
if it gets swept away beyond recall,
in spite of all the snapshots, at one stroke?

If we *are* what we remember, what are they
who don't have memories as we have ours,
who, when evening falls, have no recall of day,
or who those people were who'd brought them flowers.
The troubled conscience, though, 's glad to forget.
Oblivion for some's an inner balm.
They've found some peace of mind, not total yet,
as only death itself brings that much calm.

And those white flashes on the TV screen,
as a child, whose dad plunged into genocide,
remembers Dresden and describes the scene,
are they from the firestorm then, or storm outside?
Crouching in clown's costume (it was *Fasching*)
aged, 40 years ago, as I was, 9
Eva remembers cellar ceiling crashing
and her mother screaming shrilly: *Swine! Swine! Swine!*

The Tiergarten chief with level voice remembered
a hippo disembowelled on its back,
a mother chimp, her charges all dismembered,
and trees bedaubed with zebra flesh and yak.
Flamingos, flocking from burst cages, fly
in a frenzy with their feathers all alight
from fire on the ground to bomb-crammed sky,
their flames fanned that much fiercer by their flight;

the gibbon with no hands he'd had to shoot
as it came towards him with appealing stumps,
the gutless gorilla still clutching fruit
mashed with its bowels into bloody lumps . . .
I was glad as on and on the keeper went
to the last flayed elephant's fire-frantic screech
that the old folk hadn't followed what was meant
by official footage or survivors' speech.

But then they missed the Semper's restoration,
Dresden's lauded effort to restore
one of the treasures of the now halved nation
exactly as it was before the War.
Billions of marks and years of labour
to reproduce the Semper and they play
what they'd played before the bombs fell, Weber,
Der Freischütz, for their reopening today.

Each bleb of blistered paintwork, every flake
of blast-flayed pigment in that dereliction
they analysed in lab flasks to remake
the colours needed for the redepiction
of Poetic Justice on her cloud surmounting
mortal suffering from opera and play,
repainted tales that seem to bear recounting
more often than the facts that mark today:

the dead Cordelia in the lap of Lear,
Lohengrin who pilots his white swan
at cascading lustres of bright chandelier
above the plush this pantheon shattered on,
with Titania's leashed pards in pastiche Titian,
Faust with Mephisto, Joan, Nathan the Wise,
all were blown, on that allied bombing mission,
out of their painted clouds into the skies.

Repainted, reupholstered, all in place
just as it had been before that fatal night,
but however devilish the leading bass
his demons are outshadowed on this site.
But that's what Dresden wants and so they play
the same score sung by new uplifting voices
and, as opera synopses often say,
'The curtain falls as everyone rejoices.'

Next more TV, devoted to the trial
of Ernst Zundel, who denies the Jews were gassed,
and academics are supporting his denial,
restoring pride by doctoring the past,
and not just Germans but those people who
can't bear to think such things could ever be,
and by disbelieving horrors to be true
hope to put back hope in history.

A nurse comes in to offer us a cot
considering how bad the blizzard's grown
but you kissed your dad, who, as we left, forgot
he'd been anything all day but on his own.
We needed to escape, weep, laugh, and lie
in each other's arms more privately than there,
weigh in the balance all we're heartened by,
so braved the blizzard back, deep in despair.

Feet of snow went sliding off the bonnet
as we pulled onto the road from where we'd parked.
A snowplough tried to help us to stay on it
but localities nearby, once clearly marked,
those named for northern hometowns close to mine,
the Yorks, the Whitbys, and the Scarboroughs,
all seemed one whited-out recurring sign
that could well be 'Where everybody goes . . .'

His goggles bug-eyed from the driven snow
the balaclavaed salter goes ahead
with half the sower's, half the sandman's throw,
and follows the groaning plough with wary tread.
We keep on losing the blue revolving light
and the sliding salter, and try to keep on track
by making sure we always have in sight
the yellow Day-glo X marked on his back.

The blizzard made our neighbourhood unknown.
We could neither see behind us nor before.
We felt in that white-out world we were alone
looking for landmarks, lost, until we saw
the unmistakable McDonald's M
with its '60 billion served' hamburger count.
Living, we were numbered among them,
and dead, among an incomputable amount . . .

I woke long after noon with you still sleeping
and the windows blocked where all the snow had blown.
Your pillow was still damp from last night's weeping.
In that silent dark I swore I'd make it known,
while the oil of memory feeds the wick of life
and the flame from it's still constant and still bright,
that, come oblivion or not, I loved my wife
in that long thing where we lay with day like night.

Toronto's at a standstill under snow.
Outside there's not much light and not a sound.
Those lines from Aeschylus! How do they go?
It's almost halfway through *Prometheus Bound*.
I think they're coming back. I'm concentrating . . .
μουσομητορ ἔργανην . . . Damn! I forget,
but remembering your dad, I'm celebrating
being in love, not too forgetful, yet.

Country people used to say today's
the day the birds sense spring and choose their mates,
and trapped exotics in the Dresden blaze
were flung together in their flame-fledged fates.
The snow in the street outside's at least 6ft.
I look for life, and find the only sign's,
like words left for, or *by*, someone from Crete,
a bird's tracks, like blurred Greek, for Valentine's.

Toronto

St. Valentine's Day

Glossary

Act, The—The Prevention of Terrorism Act, a measure promulgated by the Labour government in 1974 in response to the expansion of IRA violence to the British mainland. The P.T.A. gives the British Home Secretary wide powers, including the unchallengeable rights both to detain individuals incommunicado for up to seven days and to bar citizens from entering the mainland of Britain. Originally a law requiring yearly renewal, it was made permanent under the Conservatives.

adverts—advertisements

aggro—abbreviation of 'aggression'

bevvy—slang for beverage

boot—car trunk

BR—British Rail

butties—sandwiches

chuprassie—Hindi for messenger

DIY—Do it yourself

dole—welfare

dole-wallah—The author writes: 'Wallah as in Anglo-Indian English "punkah-wallah." "The second portion of the word, *wala*, is properly a Hindi adjectival affix corresponding in a general way to the Latin *-arius"* (Yule & Brunnell, *Hobson-Jobson: A Glossary of Anglo-Indian Words and Phrases*). Though its origins are in the Raj, I have heard the expression "dole-wallah" often on Tyneside, where the word describes far too great a proportion of the population.'

'eavy—Heavy, a kind of beer favored by the macho drinker

Export A—brand of cigarettes

FA Cup—Football Association Cup, the chief trophy to be won in the British soccer season

Fasching—German Shrovetide, Mardi Gras

FED—Federation, a very strong beer from Federation Breweries in Newcastle; a favorite of the macho drinker

Full Strengths—Capstan Full Strength, a very strong cigarette

Geordies—people from Tyneside; i.e., Newcastle and environs

hinny—honey, Geordie term of endearment

hokey-cokey—a kind of street dance done in a long line

Jocks—Scots

johnnies—slang for condom

kaylied—drunk

Kim's Game—Memory game played with objects on a tray, named for Kipling's Kim

Lancaster—Allied bomber in WWII

MacGregor, Ian—Chairman of the National Coal Board, the British government body in charge of the mining industry

meths—methylated spirits, wood alchohol used by winos to lace something less strongly intoxicating

nobbut—only (nought but)

nowt—Yorkshire dialect for nought, nothing

poufy—from pouf, slang for homosexual

samosas—Indian pastries

Scargill, Arthur—leader of Britain's National Union of Mineworkers (N.U.M.)

Semper—the Opera House in Dresden

Shilbottle cobbles—High-grade coal mined in northeast England

Stoop & Scoop—Canadian motto encouraging dog owners to remove their pets' excrement from public places

tick—credit

toffee, to give oneself—complacent self-congratulation

wains—children

worlass—Geordie for my wife

yobs—derogatory term for *young men*